Table of Contents

____

INTRODUCTION

It's common knowledge that regular exercise and a balanced diet are an integral part of a healthy lifestyle. Most people believe this, indeed, every New Year great numbers of people, with the desire to make such a change to their lives, embark on new fitness or weight-loss endeavours. Yet so often, as the weeks and months roll on, the gym memberships go unused, the diets become slowly neglected and motivation (and often self-esteem with it) plummets.

Why do so many people struggle to reach their health and fitness goals? What causes them to fail?

It was these kinds of questions that were the driving force behind this book. They prompted me to look back on my own experience as both a fitness enthusiast and as a personal trainer. I have been involved in health and fitness for around twenty years and in that time I have had the pleasure of seeing many people achieve their goals. Sadly, I've seen just as many fail.

One common problem seems to be a matter of expectations. The proliferation of "quick fix" options out there is fuelling an improper mind-set for long-term fitness success. Many people want to get fit and slim right now, not understanding that lasting results take time and perseverance. Another issue I have seen is a lack of proper planning. Too often people repeat the same exercises week in, week out. After an initial boost to their health and fitness, the results begin to taper off and they become disillusioned.

For some though, the journey towards a healthier lifestyle can be even harder by the fact that they may be dealing with an injury, perhaps cannot get to a gym, or simply have no idea where to begin!

It is with these challenges in mind that I developed the Home Workout for Beginners. The training routine inside assumes no prior knowledge or skill and can be done at home with minimal equipment. It provides a structured plan that will progress gradually over six weeks.

Whatever your motivation for picking up this book; whether you want to lose excess weight, tone and shape your body, or simply increase your physical and mental wellness, you will find that this progressive exercise routine will help you achieve your goals. Be this your first, third, or thirteenth time at beginning a fitness regime, you will have all the tools you need in these pages to make this one a lasting success.

Why should you take my advice?
Well, professionally speaking, I am a WABBA certified fitness coach. I have spent time conducting group circuit-training classes and been a personal trainer, working with many people to help them burn body fat, increase strength, and build muscle. In recent years I have turned my focus to writing and publishing fitness guides, many of which have reached bestseller status on the Amazon market place.

But, it may also interest you to know that my own journey to health and fitness success was far from easy. As a kid I was somewhat slow to develop physically. Generally small and weak compared to my peers, I struggled in sports at school and in young adulthood I spent some time in the overweight category. I developed a passion for health and fitness in my early teens, inspired by Arnold Schwarzenegger.

This made me realise what the human body, with the help of correct mind-set, was capable of. I wanted to be like Arnold! In my twenties I made this dream a reality, competing in my first bodybuilding competition. In my time I've also been a long distance runner, and served a number of years in the British Army in an airborne unit (9 parachute squadron Royal Engineers). Throughout these experiences I've learned some valuable lessons from many mistakes and triumphs. In this book I draw on knowledge from both my professional and personal experiences.

Earning fitness results is not easy but my goal is to give you the key information that makes this journey as comfortable and efficient as possible. If you are up for the challenge, I am ready and waiting to help you reach your fitness and weight loss goals!

If you would like to take things a bit further and get a bit more serious I might have something for you -

Home workouts are great! Following along with the aid of pictures and words can be really rewarding but if you want to take it to the next level, you can follow along with me in real time with the *Home workout for beginners* video course!

Yes! We have made a video course based on this book!

Although the *"Homework out for beginners"* book will give you plenty of information to follow along with and give you the tools to earn great results when it comes to fitness, body toning and weight loss whilst also helping you with the mind-set and prep aspect of fitness that is vital for success, the video course will help you on a much deeper level.

If you are serious about getting real, lasting results when it comes to weight loss and body toning and you really want to change your current fitness situation, then the video course can become your ultimate guide!

All you need to do is tune in and follow along step by step!

In the video course you will have access to:

- **Mind-set Prep and planning** - The foundation of fitness success! This being the mind-set and prep part of any successful fitness endeavour. Overlooked by most people but not by you! The first module in the course will guide you through and help you plan and create your own path to fitness success.

- **At least 6 weeks of progressive exercise** - Let's do this! Starting off with basic resistance sessions using bodyweight, exercise bands and an exercise ball that progresses through the weeks in order to develop body shape, muscle strength and tone and also progressing with these exercise techniques with upgrades to resistance and cardio training.

- **Resistance training and development** - Resistance exercises are upgraded each week to build on each previous week ensuring continued development throughout the training. You will also learn why you are doing what you are doing so when you've finished the training, you will have the knowledge to design your very own workouts and have a great understanding of body mechanics.

- **Cardio training and development** - For the cardio side of the course. We will focus on fat loss and body composition change along with development of our cardio vascular system, resulting in lower resting heart rate, bigger lung capacity, lower body fat percentage and increased stamina. During your cardio sessions, you can choose to follow on a piece of home cardio equipment or with me out in the world. During these sessions I will chat to you about different topics that will further help you reach your health and fitness goals.

- **Downloadable content tools** - There are several downloadable worksheets that can be used in the planning and prep phase along with downloadable material that can be utilised in the 6 week physical training phase to help with tracking, accountability and motivation.

- **How to cook and what to eat** - Diet and nutrition is a big part of any body transformation. To this end, there are several quick and easy meal prep videos that are nutritious and balanced. You can follow along with me in the kitchen or you can take inspiration from these ideas. This is a section of the course that will be continually updated, so more healthy recipes and cooking ideas will pop up as time goes by.

- **Lifetime access** - When you sign up for the course, you will have lifetime access. This means that you can work through the course at your own pace. I actually recommend that if you get to a certain week and the upgrades are a bit tough, that you repeat the week. Although this is advertised as a 6 week long course, it can be completed in 12, 16 or even more weeks. It's important to progress with the exercise choices but consistency is arguably more important.

I could talk a lot more about the benefits of signing up for the video course but I will let you check it out for yourself and if you have any questions, please drop me an email at – Jim@jimshealthandmuscle.com

You can check this video course out HERE or head over to Yourfitnesssuccess.com for more info.

WHAT YOU WILL NEED

The start of any lifestyle change can be daunting; indeed it can be completely overwhelming if there are too many barriers in place. I've thought carefully about this when designing this programme and have made every effort to remove the most common barriers. I have considered cost, time, and convenience, and have tried to make this very affordable.

As such, this exercise plan can be done at home in a relatively short space of time, making it easy to fit into your daily routine. There are a few pieces of basic, inexpensive equipment that you will need before you begin:

- Suitable clothing and footwear:

  ✓ A good pair of running shoes. Don't panic! You won't be running in these right away, good running shoes are great for most forms of exercise.
  ✓ Outdoor clothing and high visibility jacket or strips for clothing.

- Resistance bands.

  ✓ You can buy single resistance bands, but I suggest investing in a set. A resistance band set has several different attachments and bands of varying resistance. With such a set, you will have plenty of scope for progression and effectively own a compact travel gym.
  ✓ This is the set that I used in conjunction with this routine –

- An exercise ball.
- A stopwatch or timekeeping app (Most phones have one built in)

THE ESSENTIAL ELEMENTS

The main draw to this book may be the six week training routine but there is far more value to it than just following along with the practical part. It's great that you now have a beginner home workout to follow but in my opinion, if you understand the principals behind why you are doing what you are doing, you will gain far more value from this book than you would if you simply took my word for it and followed the workouts. Most beginners to fitness will have a goal in mind, and to achieve this they tend to start with the most obvious form of exercise.

For example, if the goal is to lose weight, they might go for a run or jump on an exercise bike or even a rowing machine. If they want to gain muscle, they may grab some dumbbells and start doing some bicep curls. The problem with this common approach is that without a structured plan there will be no foundation in place to fall back on when the inevitable waves of doubt, loss of motivation, or plain tiredness, that are a part of every single fitness endeavour, come crashing in.

This six-week exercise plan is designed to guard against these common causes of fitness and weight-loss venture abandonment. By understanding the essential elements of this routine, you will have a better knowledge of how to design and plan your own workouts so you can keep progressing beyond week six.

Right now your main goal may be to lose weight, tone your body, or simply get healthy, but perhaps in the future you may want to challenge yourself further, perhaps even enter a sporting race or event. While my main aim here is to offer the novice a realistic, comfortable and non-daunting entry to fitness and exercise, I hope that it will also give you the confidence and ability to accomplish whatever fitness goal you may set your mind to.

No matter what the end goal is, be it to lose weight, run a 5K, a full marathon, or enter a body-building competition, every good fitness plan will have the following essential elements. It is the absence of one or more of these which leads so many people to give up.

Every beginner's exercise regime should be:

- **Realistic and appropriate** for your current level of fitness and skill.
- **Convenient**. It needs to fit in with your lifestyle.
- **Progressive**, challenging you more over time.
- **Planned** in advance with a schedule to follow and targets to hit.
- **Diverse**, including a good mix of cardio and resistance.

Any training plan with these qualities will provide a solid foundation upon which to build. The routine that is outlined in this book ticks all of these boxes. It will help you out all the more if you embrace a positive mind-set and stay consistent with your training.

HEALTH CHECK

Before you embark on any fitness routine, please consult your Doctor.

1. Do not exercise if you are unwell.

2. Stop if you feel pain, and if the pain does not subside, consult your Doctor.

3. Do not exercise if you have taken alcohol or had a large meal in the last few hours.

4. If you are taking medication, please check with your Doctor to make sure it is okay for you to exercise.

5. If in doubt at all, please check with your Doctor first – you may even want to take this routine and go through it with them. It may be helpful to ask for a blood pressure, cholesterol and weight check. You can then have these taken again in a few months to see the benefit.

FOOD

This book is focused on beginner exercise, which is a major part of living a healthy lifestyle. However, exercise and nutrition go hand in hand so I have put together some tips and good practices that will be highly effective when incorporated alongside your exercise routine.

Food plays a very important part in creating your body composition and fuelling your body. If you are eating too much of the wrong foods, your body composition will change accordingly. If you eat too little food, your body will work with the fuel that you have given it, making cut backs to the detriment of its function. Food and diet can be an extremely detailed subject and there are many theories and practices that seem to contradict each other. Some will claim to give you amazing weight loss or phenomenal muscle growth.

The truth is that many of these diet ideas and theories will work if they are practiced consistently. However, in my opinion, it's best to keep it simple as there is no substitute for a good knowledge of basic nutrition.

Making nutritional and dietary changes that compliment your training will help to speed up your training progression so it's worth taking note of these. With any lifestyle change, I believe that if there are too many changes going at once, it can become overwhelming.

Keeping track of a bunch of new practices can be too much of a hurdle for most and there is no need to make things more difficult than they need to be. Since an exercise routine is a large change to incorporate into your life, I would advise that you initially just make yourself aware of the food that you are eating, making only small and gradual changes when you are ready. Remember that a lot of small changes over time will result in a big change in the end.

Here are some simple ways to start building good food habits. You may want to make one of these changes every week until eventually you are practicing all of these suggestions.

- **Don't skip meals** – As a beginner, this is a good practice to help your metabolism function correctly. Eat three to four nutritionally balanced meals every day. Theories such as intermittent fasting are sound but I would advise that these practices are looked into when you become more experienced as a possible progression.

- **Drink lots of water** – Aim to drink at least two litres of water per day. Water is so crucial to our health; indeed our bodies are 50-65% water. Water is needed for numerous bodily functions. It is needed for digestion and the removal of wastes and toxins from the body. Water is vital for healthy brain and cell functioning. It helps to transport oxygen around the body and aids in the absorption of vitamins and minerals. Drinking plenty of water is one of the most basic ways you can improve your health. Conversely, sugary drinks, including sodas, energy drinks, and juices, have an extremely high sugar content. Sugar in this refined form has no nutritional benefit and will seriously hamper your weight-loss and fitness efforts. If in doubt about the make-up of any drink, steer clear of it.

- **Cut back on chocolate, sweets and desserts** – Most sticky favourites are full of sugar, fat, and generally have no nutritional value. It may seem like a boring life without some sweet treats from time to time but on the whole you will find that your health and weight-loss changes will come faster if you're also cutting down on unnecessary, nutritionally "empty" calories. Make a note of how many sweet treats you currently eat and aim to cut that down by half. If you have a sweet craving, try using this as an opportunity to train your body to gain the same satisfaction from a piece of fruit; switch out a biscuit for an orange or two.

- **Eat lean meat** – If you eat meat, always use the lean cuts for your meals. White fish, chicken, or turkey breast are a good choice. Cuts of beef with low fat content can be used occasionally throughout the week.

- **Snack on vegetables and nuts** - If you tend to snack a lot, switch out the pre-made, processed snacks for more natural ones. Try munching on raw veggies, such as carrots or celery sticks. Apple slices or mandarin oranges make great lunchbox additions, or you may want to try unsalted nuts and dried fruit for an appetite-curbing snack.

- **Add more whole grains, beans, fruits, and vegetables into your diet** – A good start is to add a portion of greens to every evening meal. Try mangetout, green beans, or broccoli. These are really easy to stir-fry and full of goodness. If you're feeling adventurous, try juicing vegetables a few times per week. Switch out white rice and pasta for their wholegrain counterparts. Try adding some fresh fruit to your breakfast cereal.

- **Slow down and eat less at each meal** – Eating smaller portion sizes is, perhaps not surprisingly, a really effective strategy for losing weight. It can be a lot easier to implement if you simply make an effort to eat slower. Many people rush through their meals, barely finishing one mouthful before stuffing the next one in. You may find it hard at first to slow down because it requires you to focus and pay more attention to your food. A good tip here is to put your knife and fork on the table after each mouthful, waiting until you have chewed and swallowed before picking them up again. Savour and enjoy every mouthful till the end. Taste the flavours and feel the textures of the food. You'll be surprised at how long a meal can last and how satisfied you can feel with less.

- **Don't cut out your favourite cheat foods altogether** – This can lead to feelings of restriction and resentment. Instead, plan to have one of your favourites only once per week. But be careful not to use this as an opportunity to binge! Moderation is key.

This is a list of things that you can work towards. I strongly advise changing just one thing at a time, rather than trying to change everything at once. Remember that we're aiming for long-lasting success here, not a quick-fix, so a gradual approach is best. By making one change per week, or even per fortnight, you will only have one thing to focus on at a time. This will lighten the load and allow time for your new healthy habits to set in.

A WORD ON MOTIVATION

To have picked up this book in the first place you must already have some degree of motivation to make a change. You may even find that during the first few days of your new fitness endeavour your motivation remains high. However, I feel that it's important to talk about motivation briefly here so that you will be better prepared for what is to come.

The beginning of any new fitness regime will require hard work and dedication. You will need to stay committed to building new healthy habits even when you become tired and your motivation begins to wane. That's the thing about motivation – it comes and goes, and this makes it an unreliable factor in fitness and weight-loss endeavours. Just being aware of this will help you to recognize when this becomes an issue for you.

It may come as a surprise to learn that some of your biggest challenges will be mental rather than a physical. For a beginner, the early stages of a new training program can be tough, as the habits and routines are not yet firmly set in place. Changing your daily life like this can be a little uncomfortable to begin with. I've been there myself and can totally empathise. However, I know that if you stay committed through this initial challenge, your training will gain momentum and you will find it easier as the days and weeks go by. Eventually you'll find it harder to stop than to keep going!

I love to think of fitness training, weight-loss ventures, or any other long-term challenge in this way; if you have "lots of a little bit of something," you will end up with "a lot". Of course, it works both ways with the human body. If you eat a few chocolate bars every day and don't burn off the extra calories, you will put on some, if not a lot, of fat. In this programme we're going to be building new healthy habits and routines.

Dramatic, overnight results are not realistic, or even healthy. Remember that long-lasting results are what we're aiming for here, not an unsustainable quick-fix. However, if you remain dedicated, you will soon see the fruits of your labour. You will start to notice the physical and mental changes in yourself. You will feel happier and more energized.

You will likely also find that the lifestyle changes that were initially so challenging are now pretty easy to keep up with. Once your new healthy habits and routines are in place they become a driving force and will keep you going even when motivation is lacking. So keep going. Force yourself to stick to the routine no matter what, knowing that once you get through this initial challenge, you will begin to gain momentum towards your goal.

On the next few pages, I have included some motivational quotes. These have been added on whole single pages so that you can cut them out if you would like some "out of the box" motivation. If, on the other hand, you would prefer to make your own, all the better.

I understand how hard it can be to get motivated at times. Right now your motivation may be high, but there will be days ahead when you find it hard to get moving, I know this because I've been there myself. At times like these I have found motivational quotes to be invaluable. Motivational quotes, or positive affirmations, that resonate with you on a personal level can really make the difference on one of those days when you are feeling low.

They can help in times of physical tiredness or mental fatigue, and they may even prevent you from making bad food choices. Having these little messages on display in your everyday life will remind you of your goals and can rekindle that fire of motivation that brought you on this path in the first place.

I suggest cutting or copying these out and placing them where you will always see them, especially in the places you will be before your training. Of course, this is by no means a definitive list. Perhaps instead you might like to make your own motivational quotes. Writing them out now before you get started is key.

Be creative – what do you think you'll want to hear when the going gets tough? I personally prefer messages with a more positive tone, rather than a hard, 'tough love' approach. Reading positive messages like this to yourself every day can really help to develop a more optimistic outlook; something which will benefit you in all areas of your life.

Get these motivational quotes pinned up before you start this routine so that they're in place when you need them. Make it a priority.

Some good places to pin up motivational quotes are:

- By the side of your bed.
- On top of your television set.
- As you walk into your house, at eye level.
- On your fridge or pantry door.
- On your bathroom mirror.
- On your monitor at work or home.

Be inventive with these quotes. If you decide to make your own, you could add photographs or pictures to the quotes. The only rule to this is that whatever you create must resonate with you. You must believe it or it will have no power to motivate you when you are feeling down.

You may find that you only need these quotes for the duration of this six-week training plan. Once you have built a solid routine you may find that you have fewer dips in motivation. However, you might find, like I have, that they continue to be useful even once you've hit your goal. You might simply want to change them up to fit your new goals. You might think this sounds too simple to be of any consequence, but don't underestimate the power of having these positive messages dotted around your life!

THINK ABOUT **WHY** YOU STARTED

YOU DON'T HAVE
TO BE GREAT
TO START

BUT YOU DO
HAVE TO START
TO BE GREAT

THE #1 REASON PEOPLE
GIVE UP SO FAST IS THAT
THEY LOOK AT HOW FAR
THEY HAVE TO GO

INSTEAD OF LOOKING
AT HOW FAR THEY'VE
GONE ALREADY...

KEEP GOING

THE ONLY
BAD WORKOUT
IS THE ONE
THAT DIDN'T
HAPPEN

LIFE BEGINS AT THE END OF YOUR **COMFORT ZONE**

ONE HOUR OF
WORKOUT

IS 4% OF
YOUR DAY

DISCIPLINE
IS THE BRIDGE BETWEEN GOALS AND ACCOMPLISHMENT

IF YOU WAIT FOR PERFECT CONDITIONS, YOU WILL NEVER **GET STARTED**

RESISTANCE TRAINING

Over the next six weeks, we will be doing two types of exercise: *Resistance* and *Cardiovascular*. Let's take a look at *resistance training* first.

Resistance training involves performing certain exercise movements against a force. This force could be in the form of barbells, dumbbells, bodyweight, or resistance bands, to name a few. For this training programme we will be mainly utilising bodyweight exercises and resistance bands of varying tensions. This will target specific muscle groups in order to improve their strength and function, and will build a solid foundation for your future training plans.

Resistance training is often underestimated, or worse still, completely overlooked by beginners. In fact, resistance training is great for burning extra calories so should form an integral part of any fitness and weight-loss program. For the purpose of this routine, you should complete any resistance training you have scheduled for the day before moving immediately on to your cardiovascular training session. In this way your resistance exercise will serve as a good warm up, also putting your body into its "fat burning zone" so you'll get the most value out of your cardio training, optimising the amount of fat burned per session.

During your first six-week training routine, you will be doing 3 - 6 resistance training sessions per week. There are a few factors that have to be considered when it comes to choosing your resistance bands or resistance level. You don't want to choose a resistance band, dumbbell or bodyweight exercise that is so tough that you can't do the movement in a controlled manner or are totally exhausted after each exercise. The point of this programme is to just get your muscles working, so we don't need a huge amount of resistance at this early stage. However, you do need to feel resistance and you need to be able to perform the exercise with reasonable comfort. I always say:

"It's not the size of the weight; it's how you lift it that counts."

So if you have a resistance band kit similar to the one I have suggested in the *"What you will need"* chapter, you should find the resistance band that is good for you on that particular exercise. You will be able to progress through the different bands as time goes by. If the lightest resistance band in the kit is still too tough, this is not a problem. You can simply do the exercises without a band at all. If this is the case, great; you will have a lot of progression to work towards and look forward to achieving. Just remember that perfecting the exercise movement is more important than adding resistance to the exercise.

It is also important to note that, at first, your resistance training sessions may feel a little awkward as you get used to the movements and find the right amount of resistance to work with. This is normal, since your muscles, including those that stabilise your body, are not used to the exercises. Don't worry, it's all part of the learning process and you will find your flow within a week or two. Just persevere and you will be surprised at how quickly you improve and these exercises start to feel smooth.

If this is your first time venturing into the world of resistance training, you may be unfamiliar with some of the terms and the format that the sessions are presented in.

Here are some terms to familiarise yourself with:

- **Reps (Repetitions)** – This is the number of times that you repeat the exercise movement within a set.

- **Sets** – This is the amount of times that you repeat a group of reps.

The main idea is that you perform several "reps" of a single exercise, have a short rest, then perform another "set" of the same exercise. Repeat until you have completed the suggested amount of sets for that exercise before moving onto the next. This is a fairly standard way of training with resistance movements and will lay a nice foundation for future training.

Here's an example of how to use the sets and reps method for push-ups:

1. Assume the starting position for a push-up. Here is the starting position of the first variation of push-up - "Push-ups on knees –

2. Lower your body towards the floor as you inhale (should take approximately 2 seconds).

3. Upon reaching the top of the movement (when your face is closest to the floor), immediately return to the starting position as you exhale (should take approximately two seconds). This is one "rep".
4. Repeat this process without stopping until you have achieved the target number of reps.
5. Once you have completed a full set of reps, rest for thirty seconds to a minute to allow your muscle group to recover before starting the next set of the same exercise.
6. Upon completion of the full amount of sets and reps for this exercise, take a thirty-second to one-minute "active rest" period before starting the next exercise.
7. During these "active rest" periods between sets, you should stand up, shake off, or gently stretch the muscle that has just been stimulated. This is why it is known as "active rest". Sitting down and relaxing will inhibit the flow of your session, making the workout less effective.

It is important to remember that each exercise targets a specific muscle group. By utilising sets and reps in this way, you will be sufficiently challenging the muscles; muscles which will play an active role in your body's ability to burn calories!

CARDIO TRAINING

Cardiovascular and aerobic training are terms used interchangeably for any exercise that increases your breathing and heart rate for a sustained period of time. 'Cardiovascular' specifically refers to the heart, whereas 'aerobic' refers to oxygen. For the purposes of this plan I will refer to these types of exercises simply as 'cardio'. Cardio is highly effective for burning calories and will, therefore, have an important place in any weight-loss program. By improving the fitness of your heart and lungs, cardio also increases your endurance.

Cardio includes activities such as running, cycling, swimming, and rowing, to name just a few. While it is a common entry exercise for many beginners to fitness, it can be easy to get it wrong. The most common mistake is trying to do too much too soon.

This can result in over-exertion, feeling sick, severe muscle soreness, or worse still, injury. I can empathise with this situation and attest to the damage it can have to your motivation and progress. If you find yourself here, please remember that it will pass and you should see it as a learning curve. Don't let it put you off, you just need to re-assess, adjust and try again.

Running and jogging is a good fat-burning exercise and it's great for heart and lung fitness, but walking at a brisk pace can be equally effective. A brisk walk that follows a resistance training session is an amazing start for any beginner. As I mentioned in the previous chapter, performing a resistance session immediately before a cardio session will optimise fat-burning. The following example explains how:

- If you go for a thirty-minute walk without previously performing a resistance session, it will take your body around ten minutes to reach a fat burning state.

- This means that within a thirty-minute cardio session only twenty minutes will be spent burning fat.

- If you perform a thirty-minute cardio session five days of the week, you will be achieving 150 minutes, or 2 ½ hours, of fat burning per week.

- If you do your resistance training before your cardio session, your body will reach a fat-burning state earlier. This means that the second you start your cardio, you will already be burning fat. This effectively gives you an extra ten minutes of fat burning per session. That's an extra fifty minutes of fat burning per week!

There are many theories and ideas about the best way to burn fat, some of these are more challenging than others. The cardio methods in this book are based on my own experience and education. I have seen this work first hand and believe that it is the best start for any beginner.
When cardio training is combined with resistance training in this way, the beginner will have a solid start to their fitness journey.

The whole body is being worked and nothing is being neglected. All major muscle groups are being targeted and a good progression of cardio exercise is being employed to ensure that a strong all-round fitness foundation is being developed. Anyone with an unshakeable foundation of this nature will have the platform to build something amazing in the future.

Although I have designed this beginner's workout routine to focus on walking and jogging as a cardio choice, I realise that this may not be an option for some. If you are unable to walk or jog for whatever reason, don't worry, there are alternatives. It may help if you consider this:

"The fat burning level that you achieve as a result of cardio exercise is based on the consistent movement of your body, the rising of your body's core temperature and the time that you have spent working at this level"

When you look at fat-burning in this light, hopefully you can see that it can be applied to many forms of movement. For instance, if you have a bicycle, or even a stationary bike set up in your home, this would be a great alternative. Swimming is another fantastic cardio option.

You could even be really creative and use a punch bag routine or simply put on some music and dance. There are plenty of exercise to music options to choose from and who knows, one day you may be able to follow me, sporting a Lycra one-piece in my very own exercise to music DVD!...although there are no plans at the moment. Joking aside, if you are stuck for ideas, I would be more than happy to give you suggestions on how to modify the routine in this book to better suit your unique situation, so please feel free to contact me via my website and I will do my best to help you out.

Whatever you decide to do for cardio, it will work if you use the same principles that I have suggested for the walking and jogging method outlined in the routine. Almost every cardio activity can be adapted to fit in with this programme. Because low-impact cardio generally requires less time for recovery, you can do it every day. You should allow for no more than one or two days off per week for the 6-week programme, although these days off are not mandatory.
If you do choose to drop cardio sessions, I suggest that these are planned for the same day every week. This will keep you more organized, focused and serve to create a good routine.

We've talked about the benefits of cardio for fat-burning and the different methods of exercise that can be employed, but how should you approach each cardio session practically to get the most out of your training?

The first thing that you need to understand is that the longer your cardio session lasts, in other words, the longer your heart rate is elevated, the more value you will get when it comes to fat-loss. The next thing you need to understand is that to be able to sustain these sessions and to make them worthwhile, the pace or tempo needs to be comfortable for you for the entire session.

This is where I tell you that everyone is different and it may take a few sessions to find your stride. Just like with the resistance exercises, it may feel a bit awkward at first. However, as you will soon see from the progressive exercise plan that follows, I have tried to eliminate the possibility of taking on too much, too soon, and have aimed to assist in a quick identification of your specific optimal training tempo.

As with resistance training, there are many different theories and methods. During this six-week training routine, the focus is on "steady state" with a sprinkle of "interval training". Here are some definitions for you:

- **Steady state:** Maintaining a constant speed that does not vary. For fat burning, the speed is normally a constant brisk walk or jog.
- **Interval training:** A mix of high and low levels of intensity. An interval training session could consist of walking, jogging and short bursts of sprints.

So, look forward to the cardio training. Find some motivating music, or audio books to listen to. Perhaps get a free running app for your phone so you can track your distance and progress. You might be surprised at how much this can help you stay motivated and focused.

D.O.M.S & MUSCLE GROWTH

The day after, or even as soon as eight hours after your first training session, you may feel a degree of pain in your muscles. This condition is known as **D**elayed **O**nset **M**uscle Soreness, or "D.O.M.S". Welcomed by many trainers, dreaded by others, one thing is for sure; if you are challenging your muscles with exercise, there is a high chance that you will experience D.O.M.S at some point.

Many people, particularly beginners mistake this pain for an injury or feel that they have done something wrong during their training session. Typically, however, this is not the case. Experiencing D.O.M.S is a natural part of training and exercise and learning how to differentiate this from a possible injury will become much easier as you progress through the programme.

The truth is that we don't know for certain what causes **D**elayed **O**nset **M**uscle Soreness. In previous years, it was widely believed that this post-workout muscle pain was something to do with lactic acid building up in the working muscle groups and was caused by a lack of stretching after the workout. This was the prevailing view when I was a beginner to fitness.

However, as our knowledge of health and fitness has grown, these ideas have evolved. The current understanding is that the D.O.M.S. is a result of 'micro tears' to the muscle fibres. To keep this as jargon-free and non-scientific as possible I will demonstrate this updated theory of D.O.M.S by using a simplified example that gives the gist of the philosophy without turning this section into a science paper.

Let's imagine that you decide to do a set of bodyweight squats. You perform the exercise with a slow and controlled movement concentrating on good range of motion and consciously targeting your quadriceps (upper, front leg muscles) throughout.

The next day, you can feel the tops of your legs aching every time you take a step or walk up a flight of stairs. They feel bruised and tender. This is a classic case of D.O.M.S. If you find yourself in this situation, this is an indication that you have performed the exercise correctly. During resistance training of this nature, the muscle suffers a small amount of damage in the form of "micro tears" in the muscle fibres. This may sound nasty but it is actually this damage that stimulates muscle growth and development.

It is believed to be these tears that cause the pain. Whenever you put a muscle through its full range of motion, you are essentially squashing it up and then stretching it out. Add some extra resistance to the movement (your bodyweight, a resistance band or a loaded barbell) and you are increasing its normal workload. It is believed that these "micro tears" occur on the extension of the muscle (when it is being stretched out). During squats, the extension happens during your downward decent to the point where your upper legs are parallel to the floor, as demonstrated in the following picture:

A lot of people actually see D.O.M.S as a benchmark for a successful training session. However, it is important that you remember the following to make sure that you get the most value from your hard work:

- If you have D.O.M.S you have essentially damaged your muscles, in doing so, you have created the catalyst for muscular development.

- Muscles need the right fuel in order to repair, so you should eat a high quality, protein rich meal immediately after training or have a quality post-workout drink that aids repair and recovery.

- Muscles need rest in order to recover, so you should aim to develop a good, consistent sleep pattern and be aware of your activity level. Activity level is a relative term, everyone is different, but for the purpose of this training guide, resistance training that targets **the same muscle group** should be done with at least one rest day between sessions. This will change as the workload and intensity increases.

- It is important to learn to identify D.O.M.S and be able to differentiate between this condition and a possible injury. If you injure yourself during training, you will generally feel pain immediately. D.O.M.S, however, will normally develop within 8 to 24 hours. If you do have pain in your joints or you are unsure about your pain, you should stop training and seek medical advice. Causing an injury is a lot worse than missing a few training sessions as you could be forced to stop training for an extended period of time. However, the gentle progression I've outline in this plan should safeguard against injury by making sure you don't do too much too soon.

- The more consistently that you train, the less intense the D.O.M.S situation will be, so if it affects you more than you would like at first, take comfort in the fact that it will get easier the more you progress and the stronger you get. D.O.M.S however is likely to be a familiar part of your fitness progression and in time you may find that you even start to measure the effectiveness of the workout by the resultant D.O.M.S.

As this is a beginner's exercise course, you should not experience extreme cases of D.O.M.S., and if you follow the exercise descriptions as I have laid out here, this will safeguard against injury. However, if you do feel very uncomfortable performing a particular exercise because of pain, leave that exercise out and resume training when the pain subsides.

If the pain persists or you are unsure about it, please consult your doctor. Remember, we want to prevent injury by making your progression gradual, so be cautious.

DEALING WITH SETBACKS

Setbacks are a natural part of life, and, therefore, an inevitable part of any fitness and weight-loss venture. Understanding this and knowing what to do when you experience your own setbacks will help you stay positive when the time comes.

How you deal with setbacks and the effect they can have on your training can vary a great deal depending on the nature of the problem or interruption. Coming back to training from injury, for example, requires a different approach to resuming training following a short-term illness, such as the common cold.

For this reason, I've split this chapter into sections that deal with each of the most common kinds of setbacks, as listed below:

1. Illness
2. Injury
3. Interruptions
4. Time restrictions

Within each section I address the concerns and questions that I have come across most often. You may find it helpful to read through all of these sections, as there are some overlapping themes.

Illness

How long should I take off from training?

Take total rest until you can resume everyday activities again without a problem. Your number one priority should be to focus on getting well. Resist the temptation to try and get back to your training too soon, as this could cause your illness to linger or even worsen. If it means that you have to spend a full week in bed to get over an illness, so be it. Stay well hydrated and eat good nutritious foods whenever possible.

Where should I pick up from?
This depends on how long you have to take off. If you have to take off between one and four weeks from your training, I recommend simply trying to pick up where you left off. It may be tempting to want to wipe the slate

clean and start again from day one, but this is often unnecessary and in reality can seriously hamper your progress. Believe it or not, your body can cope pretty well with some interruptions to training, returning to its pre-illness level of fitness relatively quickly.

If you have to take off more than four weeks from your training, I would suggest, again, first trying to pick up where you left off. If after a day or two this level seems too challenging, then try taking it back by one week in your plan. Again, you may find that it's not necessary to go back to day one. Think about it like this: setbacks are inevitable in all areas of life. If you had to go back to square one every time you met with some difficulty or interruption, you would never get anywhere!

How do I motivate myself to get back into training when I've been off for a while?

The mental challenge of returning to a routine after illness can be the hardest part for some people. If this is you, my advice to you is this:

Relax! Setbacks happen to everyone. You've already laid the groundwork so in effect the hardest part is already done. Most of the time, small setbacks such as a cold or vacation will not ruin all your progress. You'll retain some of your fitness and will find getting back into training easier than you might think. In cases where you do have to take a prolonged break from training, realize that even if you do lose some of your fitness or gain back some weight, this still does not put you back to square one. You have laid the foundation by starting on the plan and getting your body and brain used to new healthy habits, thus it'll be easier to pick it back up. It's never as hard as the first time you begin – and you've already done that!

Avoid the temptation to keep pushing back your re-start date. There's no need to be meticulous about it. Once you are well enough to be doing everyday things again you should try to resume training. There's no need to start on a Monday, or the first day of the month, or a new moon, just start as soon as your body feels well enough. You can even resume training with some minor residual cold symptoms – like a stuffy nose or the remains of a cough. Just try it. At worst, if you feel terrible and can't continue then stop and take another day.

Try again tomorrow. At best, you may find that any residual symptoms you had are alleviated and you feel better for having worked out. Take this first workout as a way of testing the waters. Even if you only manage a portion of the training session, this is still effective stimulation for your body and mind; getting muscles moving and blood flowing. It doesn't have to be a perfect session to be beneficial.

What if I find I can't continue where I left off?

As discussed above, use the first session back as a way of testing the waters. If you can't complete the whole session, don't worry; just do what you can. Tomorrow, move on to your next session regardless. Again, try this session - get as far as you can through it. If you have to stop early again, then do so. Continue on with your plan in this fashion. You'll soon find you are able to complete entire sessions again with ease and will be ready to step it up a gear. This is a much more effective re-entry into training than going back to week one!

Injury

Injuries have to be treated a bit differently to illnesses. The first steps you should take if you suffer an injury are:

- Stop your training session
- Ice the area immediately to reduce swelling
- Elevate the injured limb
- Rest the injured limb
- Seek medical advice if the injury is obviously serious or if it shows no sign of improvement within a couple of days or if pain or swelling stays or returns

How do I approach training after an injury?

It is important to allow an injury time to rest and heal. Avoid any activity that will overuse or aggravate it until it feels better, this includes at home and work. However, if possible, keep doing other activities that don't use or hurt the injury site.

When you have fully recovered from your injury and are free of pain or swelling, you can begin to reintroduce yourself to the original training plan.

The key is to go slowly. Unlike with an illness where I would advise you to simply try carrying on where you left off, with an injury, you need to be particularly cautious when reintroducing any activity that involves the injured limb. Start initially with testing the range of motion of the injured limb. Move it through its full range of motion to reduce any tightness.

Many injuries can cause a reduction of range of motion and this can become a problem later if full range is not addressed in the rehabilitation period. Gradually, with each training session, try adding a little more intensity or resistance. For example, if you injured your foot, start back first with just walking.

Keep the sessions as short as you need to initially. Build up the distance gradually over the course of a few days. Once you can complete a normal walking session, try adding a short interval of jogging here and there. Keep these intervals short to start with and pay attention to your body for the rest of the day and the following day to see if there are any delayed reactions to the activity. It may be that you need more rest between walking/running sessions for now.

What else can I do to speed up my recovery?

Nutrition is particularly important to the recovery of any injury. This is the time to be fuelling your body with the most nutrient-rich foods that you can get: Vegetables, fruit, whole grains, nuts and legumes, lean meats, and plenty of water will give your body what it needs to recover faster.

I am back to my week one level of fitness and ability now. This is so frustrating!

Recovering from an injury takes, above all, patience. You may experience feelings of self-pity, despair, and frustration. If you feel like this, take comfort in the fact that you are not alone. Even professional athletes suffer from injuries, experience the same feelings and go through the same basic recovery process. Try to focus on what you can do, rather than what you can't do. Sometimes this simple switch of focus can help you develop a much more positive attitude.

What if I can't do one of the activities in my training plan because of an injury?

As I mentioned above, focus on what you CAN do. If necessary, modify your workouts so that you can keep active in some way. If you can't run – try swimming or biking. If you can't do any sort of upper body work, focus on lower body and cardio. There's often a way to work around an injury so that you can stay fit.

Interruptions

Interruptions can be as simple as missing a couple of sessions, or they can be longer periods, like a vacation. Dealing with these kinds of setbacks is a normal part of training, so don't be hard on yourself when they happen to you.

Help! I've been on vacation and have gotten off track with my plan.

Returning to training from a vacation should be treated in much the same way as if you were returning from illness. My advice is the same in this respect so please read over that section too, but I'll briefly repeat the main points here.

Test the waters by trying to pick up where you left off. If you can only do a portion of the workout, that's fine. Leave it there and move on to tomorrow. If you need to take more rests during your workout, do so. Resist the temptation to revert back to day one of your plan. It probably won't be necessary.

If you try two or three days of picking it up where you left off and you are really struggling, then try taking it back just one week in your plan. Don't beat yourself up about having time off. Interruptions to training are inevitable, everyone goes through them, and they will not greatly hamper your overall progress if you keep a positive mind-set and jump right back into it.

Time restrictions

I don't have time for my workouts anymore. What can I do?

Sometimes in life our commitments change and we have to readjust our daily schedules to accommodate. Whatever the cause may be, finding yourself with new commitments can mean that you're no longer able to find the time for training.

There's no one-size-fits-all solution to this and besides, who am I to tell you how to organise your life? What I can tell you is this: It's a common problem, one I'm familiar with myself. My advice to you is to give yourself time to adjust to your new commitments. After a while you'll hopefully be able to see where you can squeeze in an hour of training each day. Perhaps you'll have to start getting up an hour earlier every day.

Maybe you'll wait until your baby is napping to squeeze in your workout. You may find that cycling to and from work allows you the opportunity for a decent cardio workout or perhaps you'll want to work out during your lunch break instead. Whatever your unique situation, if you can find some time each day that can be utilized for training, then you can work with that to build a great routine.

I don't have time to eat healthily anymore.

Sometimes with new commitments or time restrictions healthy eating may seem like too much effort. But if you rethink the idea of convenience foods, you'll see that natural, unprocessed foods, such as fruits, vegetables and nuts, are easy and quick to prepare. Maybe you don't have time to prepare elaborate meals at the moment, but you can still make sure that you stock your fridge, pantry and lunchbox with nutritious snacks.

Healthy meals can be quick and simple too and need not conform to the traditional ideas of what a 'dinner' should look like. Some evenings you might only have time to make a bowl of hot oatmeal with some fresh fruit and crushed almonds. That's great – it's a hundred times better for you than a microwaveable ready meal! Don't overcomplicate meal times. Think of them simply as opportunities to replenish and restore your body.

I will close this section by addressing a barrier that can often seem insurmountable and has the potential to ruin it all, yet is actually deceptively easy to break through. Upon returning from an illness, vacation, or injury, there may be a few fears and anxieties that cause you to put off that first workout; you may think that you will struggle with the training, you may feel weak, you may feel that all of your previous efforts have been wasted and you are back to square one.

These feelings are very familiar to me; I even have these feelings now when I have setbacks, and I know how hard this can be for a beginner. However, I have yet to have a negative experience upon returning to training. Once I have completed that first workout, the mental blocks are immediately lifted and I can never understand where they came from in the first place. The first training session always makes me feel positive, energised, and restores my hope and vision. Sometimes, it even feels like I have never been away!

Don't underestimate the power of a single workout, or a healthy meal, to give you a significant boost in motivation and self-esteem. If you feel that your progress has been ruined in any way, just hit that training session, eat your next healthy meal and you will be surprised at the results.

Please remember to revisit this chapter when you encounter a setback. It may be a game changer for you.

PREPARATION BEFORE YOU START

Before you start your six-week routine, it's a good idea to get yourself prepared. Correct preparation is generally overlooked but by taking the time now to plan and prepare, not only the practical aspects but your mind-set too, you will drastically improve your chances of success.

This book only scratches the surface of the planning side of things, so if you would like to go further down this rabbit hole of mind-set, planning and motivation, I have taken care of this in one of my other books – "Fitness & Exercise Motivation".

However you decide to handle your preparation, you should make sure to do at least the following:

- Pick your start date. It is important to have the start date in mind before you jump in. This will help you mentally prepare. Ensure that you have an uninterrupted 6-week period ahead of you before deciding on your start date. For example, you don't want to complete two weeks of the programme and then go on holiday for two weeks.

- Create your own motivational quotes or use the ones in this book and pin them up where you will always see them.

- Keep this book handy in your training area, grab the downloadable content if you are listening to the audio version or drop me an email and I will send you a free PDF of the workouts - (Jim@jimshealthandmuscle.com). Either way, make sure you have weeks one to six of your workouts pinned up somewhere so you can tick the boxes as you finish each workout. It's best to pin these up as if they were a calendar, so you only see one week at a time.

- Make sure you have all of the equipment that you'll need.

- Read through and familiarise yourself with the exercises. Practicing the movements beforehand will help the flow of the sessions at an early stage.

- Tell a friend or family member what you are doing and when you are starting. This should give you some extra support and you may even find a training partner to do the whole thing with. A bit of accountability goes a long way.

Make sure you have ticked off all of these before starting "Week 1".

Week 1 – 6
Exercise Plan

WEEK 1
"LET'S GET STARTED"

Resistance
Resistance should be done 3 out of 7 days per week

MON	TUES	WED	THUR	FRI	SAT	SUN

1. Seated resistance band chest press.

2 sets of 12 reps

2. Leg extensions with resistance band.

2 sets of 12 reps

3. Bicep curls with resistance band.

2 sets of 12 reps

4. Lateral raises with resistance band.

2 sets of 12 reps

5. Tricep kickbacks with resistance band.

2 sets of 12 reps

6. Crunches on floor, wrists to knees.

2 sets of 12 reps

7. Dorsal raises, hands on floor.

2 sets of 12 reps

Cardio
Cardio should be done at least 5 out of 7 days per week

MON	TUES	WED	THUR	FRI	SAT	SUN

Just walk –

- Find a route that is a 1 mile circuit, preferably one that starts and ends from your home. Although you can use a shorter or longer distance, a 1 mile circuit is a good start for most as it offers enough challenge for results and is achievable.

- Pick a landmark on this route that you believe to be around halfway. This could be a lamppost, road sign, building, or even a dip in the path. The landmark should be a permanent fixture, as it will become an important reference point in your training.

- Get into the habit of walking this route every day. Don't worry about the time that this takes at first, but do make a note of how long this walk is taking you. This first week is aimed at creating the habit as priority; any fitness benefits are a bonus.

- If you are opting for another form of cardio such as the stationary bike etc. You can use the same principals. For example - most stationary bikes these days have a digital display that you can probably set to "distance travelled", set this to 1 mile and simply pedal. Whatever cardio exercise you decide to do, make sure that you do it every day as planned. Again, it's not the amount of physical effort at this point that is important, it is the mental aspect of building the habit. If you have a specific cardio exercise that you would like to use that I have not mentioned and are struggling to adapt this, please give me a shout, I will be happy to share my ideas.

Week one is all about starting to build a strong foundation and helping with one of the most important factors in any fitness endeavour - forming a routine! There will be some physical bonuses although you may not see or feel these yet. Your body will start to function more efficiently as a result of your training; your metabolism will get to work, and you will start to burn more calories.

It is very important that you do this circuit every training day. It all starts here, so don't find excuses, just hit the sessions without fail.

WEEK 2
"KEEP IT UP"

Resistance
Resistance should be done 3 out of 7 days per week

MON	TUES	WED	THUR	FRI	SAT	SUN

1. Seated resistance band chest press.

3 sets of 12 reps

2. Leg extensions with resistance band.

3 sets of 12 reps

3. Bicep curls with resistance band.

3 sets of 12 reps

4. Lateral raises with resistance band.

3 sets of 12 reps

5. Tricep kickbacks with resistance band.

3 sets of 12 reps

6. Crunches on floor, wrists to knees.

3 sets of 12 reps

7. Dorsal raises, hands on floor.

3 sets of 12 reps

Cardio
Cardio should be done at least 5 out of 7 days per week.

MON	TUES	WED	THUR	FRI	SAT	SUN

Brisk walk around your route –

- Increase the pace of your walk without breaking into a jog or run. The pace should be faster than a normal walk but you should be able to maintain it for the duration of your cardio session. It may take a few sessions to find an ideal pace that you can comfortably maintain but this is all part of the process.

- The idea is to try to beat your quickest time from the previous week. You might be surprised at how much faster you can do this route.

- Try to beat your previous cardio session's time each day or at least match it. Don't worry if this isn't always achievable. Our main aim is to keep up a brisk walking pace all the way round, bettering your times is simply a good motivator.

WEEK 3
"GETTING INTO A ROUTINE"

Resistance
Resistance should be done 4 out of 7 days per week

MON	TUES	WED	THUR	FRI	SAT	SUN

Note the addition of an extra resistance session to this week.

1. Push-ups on knees.

3 sets of 12 reps

2. Swiss ball squats.

3 sets of 12 reps

3. Bicep curls with resistance band.

3 sets of 12 reps

4. Shoulder press.

3 sets of 12 reps

5. Tricep dips, feet on floor.

3 sets of 12 reps

6. Crunches on floor, hands on sides of head.

3 sets of 12 reps

7. Dorsal raises, hands on sides of head.

3 sets of 12 reps

Cardio
Cardio should be done at least 5 out of 7 days per week

MON	TUES	WED	THUR	FRI	SAT	SUN

A small but powerful tweak –

- By now, you will be familiar with your cardio route, you will be accustomed to seeing your chosen half-way landmark, and you should have a better understanding of your optimal pace. Don't worry if you are not quite there yet, it can take longer for some people to adjust.

- In week three, you will add a small tweak. When you reach your half-way point, you should up your pace for thirty seconds. Ideally, you should start to jog. Once the thirty seconds of elevated pace is done, you should return to your usual brisk walk for the remainder of your session.

- You may be thinking, "I have never jogged in my life!". This is a common response for many beginners to exercise but don't let this hold you back. Thirty seconds is all you need to do right now, then you can return to your normal brisk walking pace.

- By including this short jog, you will be adding a host of benefits to your fitness and health. The spike to your heart rate will cause your body to respond; since you have increased the exertion on your body, it needs to work harder to recover and in doing so will burn more calories and boost your fat-burning potential significantly for the remainder of your cardio session.

WEEK 4
"CEMENTING THE ROUTINE"

Resistance
Resistance should be done 4 out of 7 days per week

MON	TUES	WED	THUR	FRI	SAT	SUN

1. Push-ups on knees.

3 sets of 15 reps

2. Swiss ball squats.

3 sets of 15 reps

3. Bicep curls with resistance band.

3 sets of 15 reps

4. Lateral raises with resistance band.

3 sets of 15 reps

5. Tricep kickbacks with resistance band.

3 sets of 15 reps

6. Crunches on floor, wrists to knees.

3 sets of 15 reps

7. Dorsal raises, hands on side of head.

3 sets of 15 reps

Cardio
Cardio should be done at least 5 out of 7 days per week

MON	TUES	WED	THUR	FRI	SAT	SUN

Interval training –

- Start your brisk walk as you usually would. When you have been walking for five minutes, throw in a new thirty-second jog.

- Once the thirty seconds of jogging is complete, continue at your usual brisk walking pace.

- As this is a progressive routine you should not forget about the tweak that was added in week three, so once you reach your half-way marker, it's time to start another thirty-second jog.

- Once you have completed your second thirty-second jog, you should complete the remainder of your route at your usual brisk walking pace.

- You may notice that the time you spend doing your cardio sessions is starting to become a lot shorter but don't worry about this just yet. As you are adding short jogs (spikes in heart rate encouraging metabolic function) to your sessions, you will be training your body to become more efficient at fat burning.

WEEK 5
"WELL DONE! KEEP GOING"

Resistance
Resistance should be done 4 out of 7 days per week

MON	TUES	WED	THUR	FRI	SAT	SUN

1. Full push-ups.

3 sets of 15-30 reps

2. Bodyweight squats.

3 sets of 12 reps

3. Bicep curls with resistance band.

3 sets of 12 reps

4. Shoulder press.

3 sets of 12 reps

5. Tricep dips, feet on floor.

3 sets of 12 reps

6. Swiss ball crunches.

3 sets of 12 reps

7. Bent over rows.

3 sets of 12 reps

Cardio

Cardio should be done at least 6 out of 7 days per week

MON	TUES	WED	THUR	FRI	SAT	SUN

Note the addition of an extra cardio session to this week

Stepping it up –

- Start your brisk walk as usual. Continue this for five minutes and then break into a jog for thirty seconds.

- Once you finish your first thirty-second jog, continue at your usual brisk walking pace for one minute.

- When you have walked for one minute, break into another jog for thirty seconds.

- Continue this pattern until the end of your cardio training route.

- It may seem that this is a bit of a step up in progression from previous weeks but you will also notice that training in this way significantly reduces the time that you spend on your cardio training.

WEEK 6
"CONGRATULATIONS!
FIRST SIX WEEKS OF FITNESS DOWN"

Resistance
Resistance should be done 4 out of 7 days per week

MON	TUES	WED	THUR	FRI	SAT	SUN

1. Full push-ups.

3 sets of 15-50 reps

2. Bodyweight squats.

3 sets of 25-50 reps

3. Bicep curls with resistance band.

3 sets of 25-50 reps

4. Shoulder press.

3 sets of 25-50 reps

5. Tricep dips, feet on floor.

3 sets of 25-50 reps

6. Swiss ball crunches.

3 sets of 25-50 reps

7. Bent over rows.

3 sets of 25-50 reps

Cardio
Cardio should be done at least 6 out of 7 days per week

MON	TUES	WED	THUR	FRI	SAT	SUN

Another jump –

- Start your brisk walk as usual. Continue this for five minutes and then break into a jog for thirty seconds.

- Once you finish your first thirty-second jog, continue at your usual brisk walking pace for one minute.

- When you have walked for one minute, break into another jog for thirty seconds.

- Continue this pattern until the end of your cardio training route.

- Once you reach your usual finish point, you should repeat the whole thing so you are effectively doubling your distance.

- You have a choice at this point; You can either complete your second "lap" as you completed your first, by maintaining the pattern of thirty-second jogs followed by one minute of brisk walking. This choice will give you a cardio session covering a distance of two miles and using a full interval training method. The session will be good enough for a sustainable fitness plan for the long-term and you should see a good rate of fat burning as a result.

- Your second choice is also a viable one; you could choose to complete your second lap at a brisk walking pace with no extra jogging stints. This will lengthen the time that you are spending on your cardio session but still give you a good level of fat burning potential.

- At this point, you may notice that your cardio sessions are taking more or less the same amount of time as they were in week one, but look at how much extra value you are now getting and note at how much you have improved. This is life-changing stuff!

Although you have now reached the end of your first six-week training course, there is still room for improvement and you should always look to tweak things here, challenging yourself a little more as time goes on.

Perhaps the more important things about this six-week training routine, more important than the type of training you have been doing, are the development of habits, establishing a routine, and seeing a degree of results. These things really are the foundations of your fitness and weight-loss success. Once you have this in place, you may want to look into training for an event, such as a 5K, or you may want to ease off on the running and spend more time working with resistance methods such as circuit training, who knows, perhaps even bodybuilding! There's a whole world of fitness development options waiting for you.

WHAT DO YOU THINK SO FAR?

I am always eager to hear what you think of my exercise routines.

I would really appreciate it if you left a review and rating on the online retail store from which you made this purchase and tell others about your experience.

Please take a few moments to do this if you have enjoyed this book so far.

Thanks for the feedback! ☺

Exercise Descriptions

Seated Chest Press
Start Position

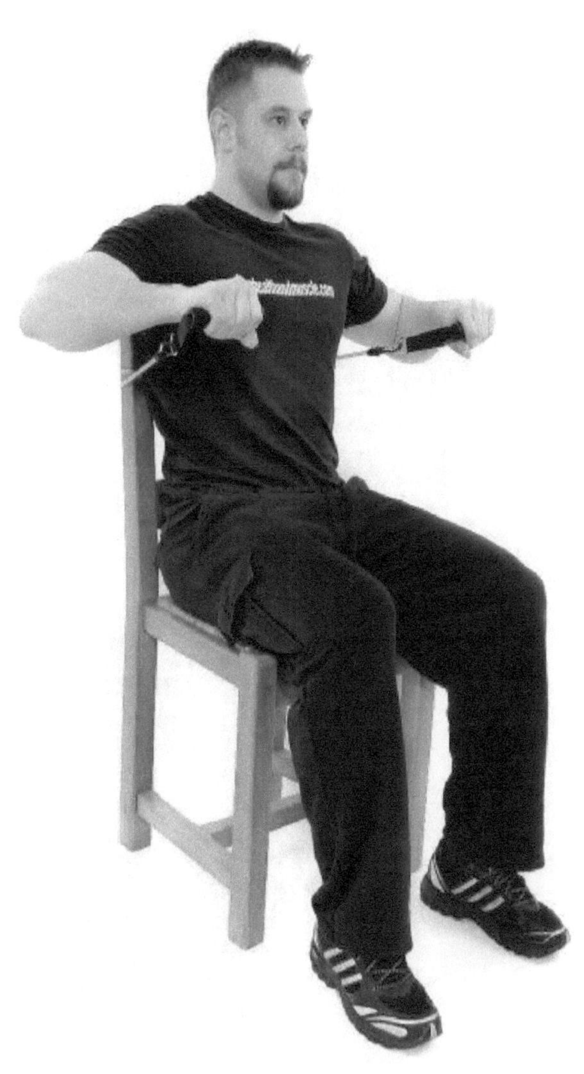

Top of Movement

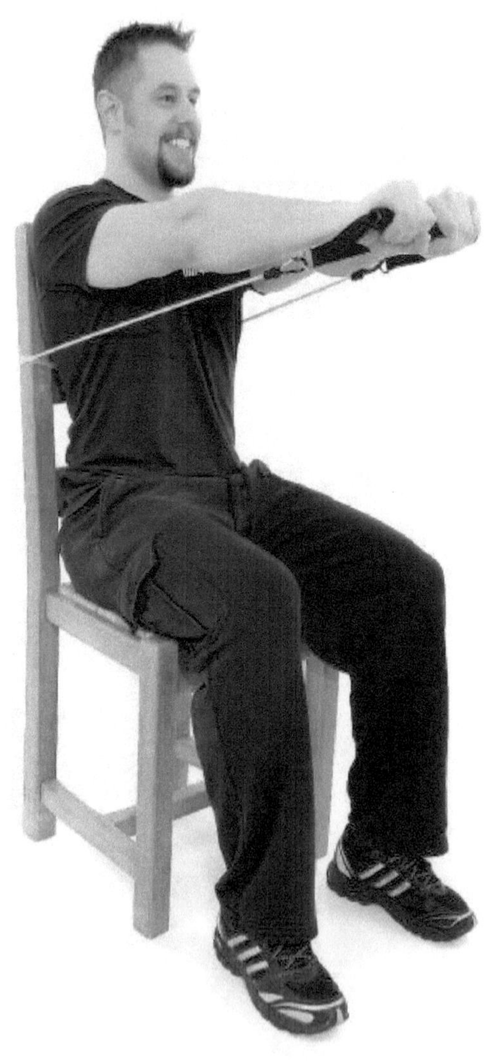

DESCRIPTION OF EXERCISE (SEATED CHEST PRESS)

Attach stirrups to each end of the band. Cross the band around a high back chair (See more info section).

Start position: Sit on the chair with the band attached ensuring that your back is straight, your feet are flat to the floor and you are looking straight in front of you. Hold the stirrups in each hand with palms facing the floor ensuring that your forearms are parallel to the floor. Your hands should be in line with your chest and you should feel a slight resistance from the band.

Movement: Keeping your forearms parallel to the floor, straighten your arms out in front of you and bring your hands to meet each other at the end of the movement so they touch when your arms are fully extended. You should also exhale as you do this.
Return to the start position whilst breathing in and you have completed one rep. You should feel this in your chest.

Leg Extensions
Start Position

Top of Movement

Description Of Exercise
(Leg extension)

Attach the ankle straps to both ends of the band (See more info section).

Starting Position: Sit on a chair or bench, Place one end of the resistance band either under your left foot or wrapped around the rear right chair leg. Attach the ankle strap around your right ankle. If you do not have one of these you can make a loop in the band. Grasp sides of chair with your hands for support. Keep the toes on the foot of your working leg pointed up.

Movement: As you exhale, extend your right leg to the point just before you lock out, try to get your lower leg parallel to the floor. From this point, keeping your leg straight, lift your upper leg towards the ceiling.
Return to the start position by bending your knee whilst breathing in. This completes one rep. Finish your set and swap legs.

Bicep Curl
Start Position

Top of Movement

DESCRIPTION OF EXERCISE
(BICEP CURL)

Attach stirrups to each end of the band.

Start position: Hold a stirrup in each hand, step forward with one foot securing the middle of the band under the rear foot. Keep your palms facing forward and allow your arms to fall naturally at your sides with elbows slightly bent, eyes looking straight and your back flat.

Movement: Whilst breathing out, bring your forearms up to as parallel with your upper arm as possible and squeezing your bicep.
You should not rotate your palms inwards. Your palms should be facing the front of your shoulder at the top of this movement (Maximum contraction). Breathe in as you return to the starting position.
This completes one rep. You should feel this in your biceps, the front of your upper arm.

Lateral Raises
Start Position

Top of Movement

DESCRIPTION OF EXERCISE
(LATERAL RAISES)

Attach stirrups to each end of the band.

Start position: Hold a stirrup in each hand, step forward with one foot securing the middle of the band under the rear foot. Keep your palms facing inwards, your elbows slightly bent and locked, eyes looking straight and your back flat.

Movement: Whilst breathing out and keeping your elbows and wrists locked, bring your arms parallel or just above parallel to the floor. Breathe in on returning to the start position. This completes one rep. You should feel this in your shoulders.

Tricep Kickbacks
Start Position

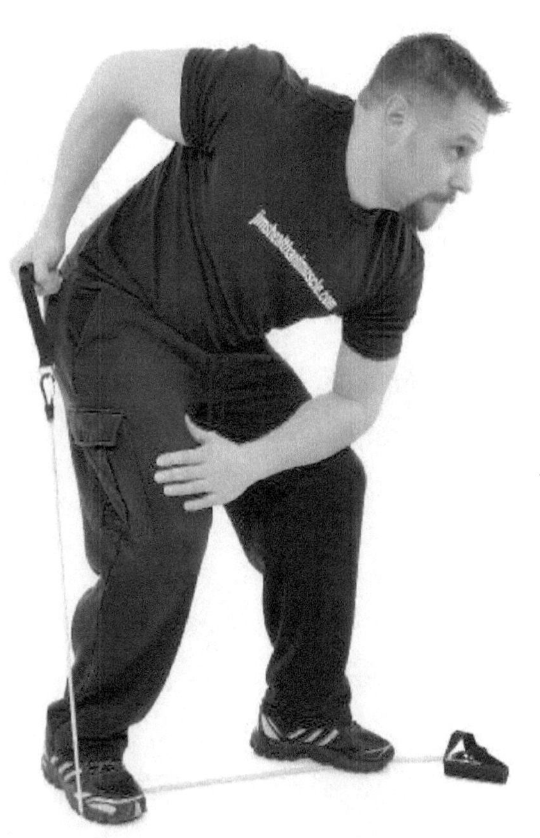

Top of Movement

DESCRIPTION OF EXERCISE
(*TRICEP KICKBACKS*)

Attach stirrups to each end of the band.

Start position: Place the exercise band on the floor and step on it around 12"
from the stirrup attachment with your right foot, this will be your front foot.
(This will vary from person to person. You are looking to have tension on the
band at the starting position). Bring your left foot behind you to give yourself
a good platform.
Keep your knees bent and your feet where they are.
Bend over to pick the stirrup up with your right hand. Stay bent over with a
flat back and pull your upper arm to your side and keep your elbow in. You
should by now feel the tension from the band. If you don't, bring your right
foot closer to the stirrup.
Twist your palm so it is facing forwards.

Movement: Keeping your upper arm parallel with the floor and your palm
facing forwards, whilst breathing out, move your lower arm towards the sky
to the point just before it locks out. Then bring this back to the starting
position as you breathe in, this completes one rep.
Once the set is done switch arms. Do the same thing again with your left foot
leading.

Crunches Wrists to knees
Start Position

Top of Movement

DESCRIPTION OF EXERCISE (CRUNCHES WRISTS TO KNEES)

Start position: Lay flat on your back and bring your knees up so that your feet are flat on the floor, about shoulder width apart. Place your hands on your thighs.

Movement: As you breathe out, slowly lift your upper body off the floor whilst sliding your palms towards your knees. You should aim to get your wrists to your knees. Once at the top of this movement, breathe in and lower your upper body back to the start position. This completes one rep.

Dorsal Raises Hands on Floor
Start Position

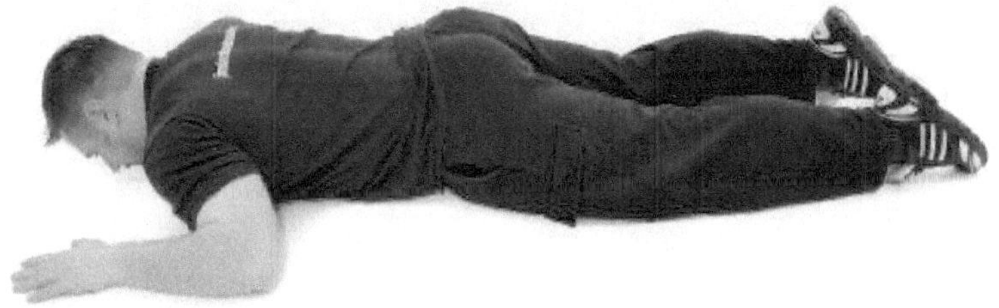

Top of Movement

DESCRIPTION OF EXERCISE (DORSAL RAISES HANDS ON FLOOR)

Start position: Lay face down on the floor, pointing your toes so the tops of your feet are also in contact with the floor. Your forearms should be in contact with the floor and at right angles to your upper arm with palms facing down.

Movement: As you breathe out bring your upper body off the floor assisting slightly with your hands. Once at the top of the movement, lower your upper body in the same way whilst breathing in. This completes one rep. (It is important to remember that this is a small range of movement so don't strain yourself too much at the top of the movement.)

Push-ups On Knees
Start Position

Top of Movement

DESCRIPTION OF EXERCISE
(PUSH-UPS ON KNEES)

Start position: Get into a position on the floor on your hands and knees. Your
Hands should be about shoulder width apart and in line with your face.

Movement: Keep your back straight and lower your upper body towards the floor by bending your elbows and breathing in.
Once you're at the bottom of this movement, raise your upper body back to the starting position whilst breathing out. This completes one rep. If you can do more than 30 of these, move to full push ups.

Swiss Ball Squats
Start Position

Top of Movement

DESCRIPTION OF EXERCISE
(SWISS BALL SQUATS)

Start position: Stand with your back against a flat wall, then position the ball in between your back and the wall so it rests in your lower back.
Keep your feet hip-width apart, slightly in front of your shoulders.

Movement: As you breathe in, bend your knees until your quads (thighs) are parallel to the ground. (The exercise ball will roll and end up between your shoulder blades).
Then push back through your heels to the starting position whilst breathing out.
Ensure that you are always looking straight ahead or slightly up. This will help you keep good posture. This completes one rep.

Shoulder Press
Start Position

Top of Movement

*note; please skip this exercise or check with your doctor if you have a known heart condition.

DESCRIPTION OF EXERCISE
(SHOULDER PRESS)

Attach stirrups to each end of the band.

Start position: Hold a stirrup in each hand, step forward with one foot securing the middle of the band under the rear foot. Keep your palms facing forward and in line with your chin. Your eyes should be looking straight and your back should be flat.

Movement: Whilst breathing out and maintaining your posture, push the stirrups above your head as high as you can bringing the two stirrups together to touch at the top of the movement. You should not let your elbows lock. As you breathe in, lower your arms back to the starting position. This completes one rep.

Tricep Dips Feet on Floor
Start Position

Top of Movement

Description Of Exercise
(Tricep dips feet on floor)

(For this exercise I would make sure the chair or bench is against a wall so it does not slip).

Start position: Sit with your back to a bench or chair and place your hands so that your fingers are pointing forward and taking your bodyweight.
You should now be in an elevated seated position with your feet flat on the floor.

Movement: As you breathe in, lower your body allowing your elbows to flare out naturally to the side as you lower your body towards the floor. You should lower yourself only to the point that you feel the stretch on your triceps (the back of your upper arms). Once at the bottom of the movement, raise your body back up to the starting position as you breathe out. This completes one rep.

Crunches Hands On Side Of Head
Start Position

Top of Movement

Description Of Exercise
(Crunches hands on side of head)

Start position: Lay flat on your back and bring your knees up so your feet are flat on the floor about shoulder width apart. Place the tips of your fingers on the sides of your head.

Movement: As you breathe out, slowly lift your shoulder blades off the floor until you feel your abdominal muscles tighten into a full crunch. Keep your lower back in contact with the floor.
Once at the top of this movement, breathe in and lower your upper body back to the start position. This completes one rep.

Full Push-ups
Start Position

Top of Movement

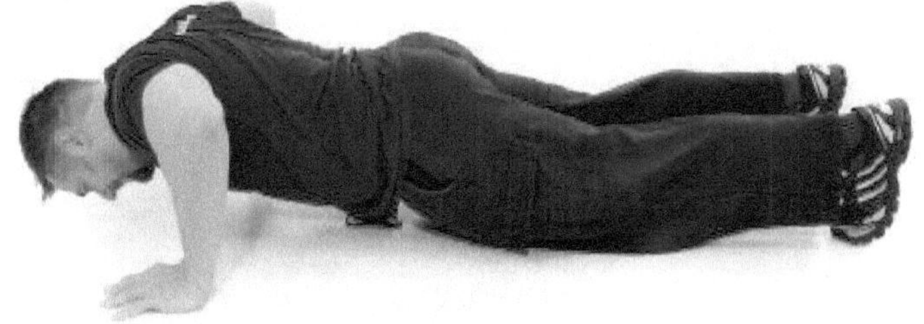

Description Of Exercise
(Full push-ups)

Start position: Get in to a position on the floor so that your hands are about shoulder width apart and in line with your mid/upper chest. You should keep your back flat and take the weight of your body. Make sure that you do not dip your head.

Movement: Keep your back straight and lower your upper body towards the floor by bending your elbows whilst breathing in. Once you are at the bottom of this movement, as you breathe out raise your upper body back to the starting position. This completes one rep.

Bodyweight Squats
Start Position

Top of Movement

Description Of Exercise
(Bodyweight squats)

Start position: Stand with your feet hip-width apart, toes slightly turned out and your arms across your chest. Focus on a point on a wall or in the distance that is eye-level or higher and look at this throughout the movement. This will help you keep your posture and maintain correct form.

Movement: Keeping your feet flat on the floor, as you breathe in, bend your knees until your quads (thighs) are parallel to the ground. Push back through your heels to the starting position, whilst breathing out. Ensure that you are always looking straight ahead or slightly up. This will help you keep good posture. This completes one rep.

Tricep Dips Heels On Floor
Start Position

Top of Movement

Description Of Exercise
(Tricep dips heels on floor)

(For this exercise I would make sure the chair or bench is against a wall so it does not slip)

Start position: Sit with your back to a bench or chair and place your hands so that your fingers are pointing forward and taking your body weight.
You should now be in an elevated seated position with your feet flat on the floor. Stay in this position but straighten your legs out in front of you so that your heels are on the floor and toes are pointed up.

Movement: As you breathe in, lower your body allowing your elbows to flare out naturally to the side as you lower your body towards the floor.
You should lower yourself only to the point that you feel the stretch on your triceps. (the back of your upper arms). Once at the bottom of the movement, push your body back up to the starting position with your arms, as you breathe out. This completes one rep.

Swiss Ball Crunches
Start Position

Top of Movement

Description Of Exercise
(Swiss ball crunches)

Start position: Sit on the swiss ball with your feet flat on the ground. Walk your feet forward so the swiss ball rolls up your back and you are in a lying position. The swiss ball should be in your mid to lower back and you should be looking up at the sky.
Place your finger tips on the side of your head.
DO NOT CLASP YOUR HANDS BEHIND YOUR HEAD.

Movement: Keeping your feet flat on the floor, you should lift your shoulder blades up, this will put immediate tension on your abdominals. You should breathe out as you do this.
Your lower back should not lose contact with the swiss ball and your eyes should be in line with the sky at a 45 degree angle. Once you reach the top of the movement, lower your shoulders to the starting position, whilst breathing in. This completes one rep.

Bent Over Rows
Start Position

Top of Movement

Description Of Exercise
(Bent over rows)

Attach the stirrups to both ends of the band, loop through the door attachment (See more info section).

Start position: Stand with your feet shoulder width apart, bend over so your upper body is just above parallel to the floor and your back is straight. Bend your knees just slightly. Take up the slack of the resistance band so that you have tension when your hands are in front of your body, as illustrated.
Keep your head up and look forward at all times.

Movement: As you breathe out, pull the bands in to your body, I always aim for my belly button *"When you row, stay low"*. Once at the top of the movement, return to the start position as you inhale. This completes one rep. Remember to keep your head up, chest out and back flat throughout the movement.

More Information

More info: Chest press
Position 1

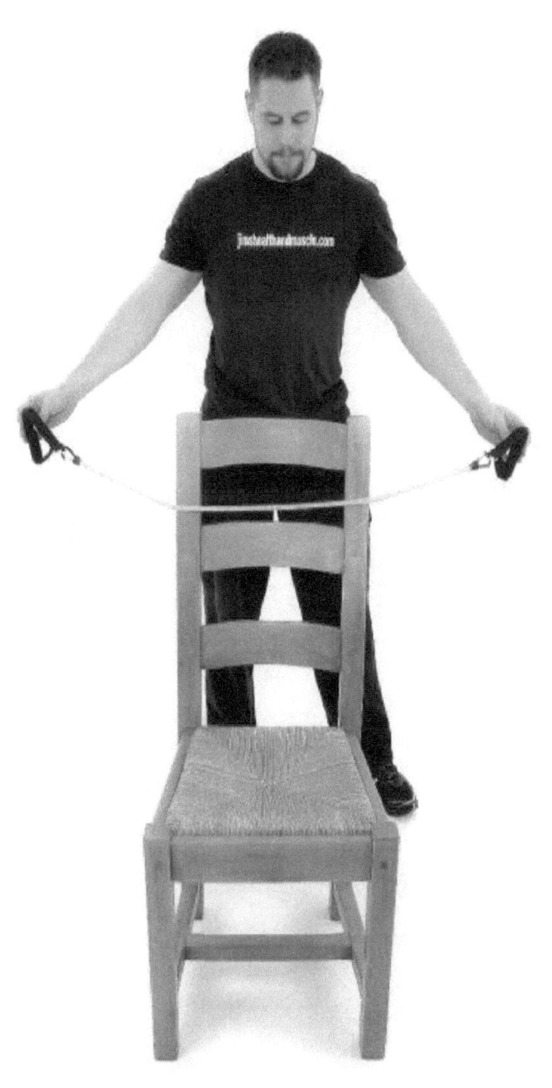

Position 2

Description

- Attach the stirrups to both ends of the band
- Position 1 :Loop the band around the back of the chair
- Position 2: Cross the exercise band over at the back of the chair

More info: Leg extensions

Description

- Attach a stirrup to one end of the band and an ankle strap to the other.
- Position 1: Place the stirrup through the front chair leg.
- Position 2: Pass the exercise band around the opposite front leg and continue to wrap around the rear chair legs until the ankle strap meets the front stirrup.
- (Note that this example shows the set up for right leg training only)

More info: Bent over rows

Description

Attach the stirrups to both ends of the band, loop through the door attachment.

Before you start the exercise, ensure that you have even lengths of exercise band on each side of the door attachment.

This picture shows the door attachment that came with my exercise band kit. Different kits will have varying attachments.

When using these attachments, ensure that you are using a closed door that opens away from your working position. This will give extra stability.

Where Do You Go From Here?

Now that you have introduced a home workout routine into your life and hopefully established a good set of habits that will enable you to develop the body and weight goals of your dreams, you do not have to sit back on your laurels, you can step it up a gear and get your results even quicker!

I have written a follow up to this book that will push your fitness to the next level. This exercise routine can also be done from the comfort of your own home.

I have designed the next six week routine to run as a nice challenging progression to the routine outlined in this book by introducing a different method of training.

The next book in this series is called:

"Home workout circuit training"

The routines from "Home workout circuit training" use a fusion of cardio and resistance training to demonstrate a whole new way of utilizing some of the movements already learned in this book.

Training in this way can massively boost your muscle strength and tone, while also making a huge difference to your fat burning goals! Home Workout Circuit Training offers a smooth and fitting transition from the methods of training outlined in this book to a whole new boost in fitness and weight-loss progression; it can be a lot of fun and circuit training also offers a huge amount of scope for personalization.

Having a solid physical training routine that offers progression in place is great if you are looking to achieve real fitness results, whether this be fat-loss or muscle toning, or general health and fitness. But the physical aspect of fitness training and progression is only part of the puzzle. If you are someone that has no problem sticking to a training routine, has the willpower to easily stick to a diet, and has the mental robustness to keep going when the hurdles keep stacking up, all you need to do is get out there and make it happen.

But what about the rest of us? Yes, the mental aspect of any kind of fitness, diet or lifestyle change can be more challenging than the physical and I believe that if the beginner decides to take up the challenge of a fitness or weight-loss venture and wants the best chance of success, that they should invest in the correct mental preparation as a priority.

I believe in this so much so that I have written a book based on these principals. "Fitness & Exercise Motivation" was inspired by some of emails I received from readers of this book. I absolutely loved writing this book as it allowed me to engage with readers. Hearing of their struggles and challenges made me realize that I had experienced much of the same and this prompted me to draw from aspects of my personal journey, thus creating a useful guide for the development of a winning mindset.
"Fitness & Exercise Motivation" has connected me with many interesting people and I have made some great new friends from this book, which both humbles me and makes me grateful. The book has been a best seller on the US Amazon store and continues to carry the "Bestseller" sticker on the UK store at the time of writing.

If you are like I was in the past, if you have struggled with motivation and have not made a conscious effort to spend time cultivating the right mindset for fitness success, I hope that you will find the following excerpt from Fitness & Exercise Motivation" useful:

"FITNESS & EXERCISE MOTIVATION

CHAPTER 6

MENTAL CHALLENGES

When it comes to the subject of fitness training and healthy lifestyle changes, most people look at the physical aspect of the new undertaking as being the most challenging aspect that they need to overcome.

But, as I explained earlier, this is not true. I can assure you that the mental challenges of any exercise routine or diet are by far the hardest hurdle to overcome.

When it comes to dieting and training, I truly believe that the mental challenges, when compared against those of the physical, are 90% of the entire struggle. Your physical challenges just measure up to about 10% of the whole barrier structure.

In Winter of 2001, I was fully in the military. I had passed my basic army training and also finished my combat engineer training. During our basic training, we had all been asked if we were interested in taking the tests to serve with 9 Parachute Squadron Royal Engineers or 59 Independent Commando Royal Engineers.

At the early stage of our training, many of our guys put their names forward since there was a stigma attached to anyone who was wearing a maroon or green beret. These guys were (and still are) viewed as the hardest soldiers in the Royal engineers who always get the first opportunity to get into the action. These guys were viewed as highly professional machines who could be phased by nothing. Of course, when you are a new recruit, you are very optimistic and pretty naive and your outlook is, "How difficult can it be?"

Consequently, about 60% of my group put their names forward to be considered for the ranks of these "special forces" kind of guys.

By the middle of the second phase of our training, we were all asked the same question, and this would be the point that anyone wanting to test for 9 Para Squadron or 59 Commandoes would have to officially sign up for it. At this point, everyone who had lasted the basic training and second phrase training so far had a pretty good idea of how hard this could get. Only three of us signed up for 9 Squadron.

When the day finally came, we had passed out as trained combat engineers and wore our blue berets with pride (later in my army career, I would learn to call this a "crap hat"). All the recruits who passed were sent to different postings; some went north, some south and some to Germany. The three of us who had volunteered for 9 Squadron got posted right into the wolf pack in Aldershot to start the pre para selection process also known as the "Beat-Up Course."

For a new recruit and a "crap hat," 9 Squadron is a pretty hostile place to be.

Previously, we had only seen the odd one or two maroon berets walking around, and these guys gave off plenty of attitude, but now all there was were maroon berets. Most of the guys didn't even acknowledge us; some quizzed us on who we were and what we were doing here in all but friendly manner.

The beauty of this selection process is that the applicant can quit at any time, and admit that this type of soldiering is not for him. Until an airborne soldier passes the rigors of "P Company," completes his parachute jumps training and accepts his parachute wings, he is not obliged to stay.

On every training session during the beat-up course, the squad of potential future airborne solders is followed by a Land Rover. This is known as "The Jack Wagon." If an applicant is injured, passes out or just decides that he's had enough, he can jump on-board, sit down and chill out. But if he gets on the Jack wagon willingly, it will be the end of his time with the airborne forces.

This fact makes it a lot easier for the applicants to throw in the towel. And coupled with the outrageously tough physical aspect of the course, it is under this psychological pressure that an applicant is tested on their mental robustness.

Early every morning of the beat-up course, about fifteen of us would form up in three ranks outside the barracks block ready for the first training session of the day. It would be the three of us from my basic training intake who were the *newbies* to this course. The rest of the other applicants ranged from having served one or two years in the army and having ranks of lance corporal to even more experienced veterans of eight plus years, sporting ranks of Sergeant.

The first training session of the day was always a straight-up run or a weighted march or run with boots and weapon. We would set off from the barracks and head towards the training area. These sessions were, at least, an hour and thirty minutes. Anyone who has been to the training area in Aldershot will know that, when I say *training area*, I don't mean a simple running track. There were countless hills in this zone and a lot of them had names, "spiders," "sisters" and "flagstaff," to name a few. The ground was uneven and ran around several different environments. There was loose, rocky terrain, lots of potholed and puddled areas, and there was even a big stretch of sand that lived up to its name of "Long valley."

Every day, the training staff would try to break us mentally and physically, and, because the option to quit was always available, it was not uncommon to run with a partner in the morning and find them gone by afternoon, never to be seen again.

On one such occasion, we had set off on our usual run. It was a particularly hard run that saw us starting with and maintaining an unusually fast pace. It took us through hill sprint reps, firemen's carry hill reps, and through our fair share of water and mud.

Everyone struggled through this training session, but there were a certain few who struggled especially. One guy, in particular, spent most of his time at the back of the squad and needed constant encouragement throughout the session. He was last on all of the hill reps and carries, fell behind regularly and had to play catch up, but he stuck with it.

Even though this guy struggled the most throughout the training session and was repeatedly offered the comfort of the Jack wagon, he kept going. This is the quality of mental robustness that the para training staff are looking to harvest.

As this training session was several weeks into the beat-up course, we knew the area and knew when the session was finally coming to an end. We had all been pushed to our limits and were ready to get back to the showers and refuel for the next beating. When we were about 0.5 miles from the barracks, the guy who had struggled so much appeared to be finding his stride and had fallen in with the rest of us.

As the barracks front gates came into view, I must admit that the sight of steel mesh and barbed wires had never looked so inviting. *That was our finish line!* It was only twenty feet away and the feeling of accomplishment was mutually shared by everyone in the squad. Everyone was running tight and together as one triumphant unit including the guy who had struggled so much. Ten feet, five feet closer, but the staff kept on running past the gate!

The session was not over. No more than ten feet past the gate, not only did the guy who had struggled so much earlier stop dead in his tracks, but other guys started to drop back, too. The whole mood of the squad plummeted from high and triumphant to low and unhopeful.

The pace of the run did not drop, which subconsciously turned the physical challenge into a mental and physiological battle that each man had to fight on his own. This was made even harder when one of the staff dropped back to the side of the now scattered squad and announced,

"Never assume that it's over and you'll get on a lot better on this course."

This did affect me mentally, but I was able to overcome and quickly accept that it wasn't over until I decided that it was. I stuck with the training staff as I had done through the training session and held on.

We did not go back onto the training area, we merely ran to the next gate of the camp and finished at this one. It was about two hundred meters away. In that time, we had lost two of the squad to the Jack wagon.

In my opinion, this is a crying shame because it was a mental failure and not a physical one. The guys who quit and rewrote their futures at this point were victims of mental defeat rather than the expected physical failure.

These guys effectively reshaped their futures by making a conscious decision to give up. It was the thought of the unknown that stopped them. If the staff had told them that we would just be going to the next gate, they would, no doubt, have flown through. Even if they were asked to sprint to the gate, I believe they would not have had much of a problem in doing so.

For the sake of two hundred meters of the unknown, these guys would never earn a maroon beret. This was the first time that I realised that developing mental robustness can be the make or break of well laid-out plans, especially with a fitness routine or diet plan.

I am aware that this might represent an extreme account of a mental challenge, but I assure you that it is not too different from the types of challenges a beginner to fitness may encounter. I learned a lot of lessons from this one training session, but it is only until recently that I began to see it in a new light, in more detail and broken it down enough that I can actually liken this single training experience to that of a long term fitness or fat loss journey.

I know the feeling of starting from the beginning of a fitness project and, as I have mentioned in previous chapters of this book, I believe that this is the hardest part. The longer that you stick with it, the easier that it gets. But you have to be aware that it is not just a physical challenge.